Debt and the Profitability of
Foreign-Controlled Domestic Corporations
in the United States

by

Harry Grubert*

OTA Technical Working Paper 1

July 2008

OTA Technical Working Papers is an occasional series of reports on the research, models and datasets developed to inform and improve Treasury's tax policy analysis. Views and opinions expressed are those of the authors and do not necessarily represent official Treasury positions or policy. *OTA Technical Working Papers* are distributed in order to document OTA analytic methods and data and invite discussion and suggestions for revision and improvement. Comments are welcome and should be directed to the authors.

`Office of Tax Analysis
U.S. Department of the Treasury
1500 Pennsylvania Avenue, NW
Washington, D.C. 20220

* U.S. Department of the Treasury. Harry.Grubert@do.treas.gov

---

The author is grateful to Geraldine Gerardi, Bill Strang and Patrick Driessen for very helpful comments. Michael Cooper and Portia Defilippes provided tabulations and prepared the data file. The views expressed in this paper are those of the author and do not necessarily represent those of the U.S. Treasury Department.

Abstract

Abstract: U.S. corporations controlled by foreigners continue to report lower net income in relation to total receipts than comparable domestically-controlled corporations. But the 2004 tax return data show that, in manufacturing and the entire nonfinancial sector, the discrepancy disappears when using a measure of operating income that focuses on the corporations' activities in the United States. To determine operating income, dividends, interest and royalties are subtracted from net income and interest paid, depreciation, amortization, and depletion are added back to net income. Domestically-controlled corporations receive much greater dividend and royalty income, mainly from their subsidiaries abroad.

In the nonfinancial sector, foreign-controlled U.S. corporations do not on average pay a larger percentage of their cash flow in interest than their domestically-controlled counterparts. They are also less likely to have very high levels of interest expense, using 50 percent of cash flow as the threshold.

Foreign-controlled U.S. corporations in finance, insurance, and real estate exhibit a wide range of profitability compared to similar domestically-controlled corporations. For example, foreign-controlled corporations in real estate are on average much more profitable than domestically-controlled real estate corporations. On the other hand, foreign-controlled property and casualty insurance corporations and securities dealers and investment banks report modest income compared to domestically-controlled corporations.

In finance, foreign-controlled commercial banks and securities dealers and investment banks pay more interest than domestically-controlled corporations as a percentage of cash flow. They are also much more likely to have very high levels of interest expense relative to cash flow. For example, the probability that a domestically-controlled securities dealer and investment bank pays more than 90 percent of cash flow in interest is less than 5 percent but greater than 40 percent for comparable foreign-controlled U.S. corporations.

1

Debt and the Profitability of Foreign-Controlled Domestic Corporations in the United States

Foreign-controlled domestic corporations (FCDCs) in the United States have the opportunity to reduce their U.S. taxable income by increasing their reliance on debt or by distorting the prices of intercompany transactions with related parties abroad. Like U.S. based multinational corporations, their intercompany transfer prices are governed by section 482 of the Internal Revenue Code and its associated regulations. In addition, section 163(j) of the Internal Revenue Code may limit the deductibility of "excess interest expense" on loans from related parties not subject to U.S. tax if the corporation's ratio of debt to equity exceeds 1.5 to 1.

The possibility that FCDCs in the United States may be improperly reducing their U.S. taxable income is suggested by data that show that, historically, they have been relatively unprofitable compared to domestically-controlled corporations (DCCs). The persistence of this low relative profitability of FCDCs is shown on Figure 1, which is derived from data from corporate income tax returns for 1995 through 2003 and that are published in annual articles in the *Statistics of Income Bulletin.*[1] The profitability measure used in the comparison is the ratio of net income to total receipts.[2] These data show that over this period large FCDCs in manufacturing and the nonfinancial sector as a whole were consistently less profitable than large DCCs. For most of these years, FCDCs in the financial sector were also less profitable than their domestic counterparts.

---

[1] http://www.irs.gov/taxstats/article/0,,id=96311,00 html#2.
[2] Net income is total income less total deductions before 'special deductions' and net operating losses. Total receipts include all of the income received by a corporation and reported on its tax return, including gross receipts before the deduction for cost of goods sold and business expenses, and interest on tax exempt obligations. Large corporations are those with assets of $250 million or more and/or business receipts of $50 million or more. Foreign-controlled domestic corporations are those with 50 percent or more foreign ownership. The data exclude real estate investment trusts, regulated investment corporations, S corporations and corporations with foreign ownership between 25 and 50 percent.

A more detailed examination of the profitability difference in 2004 (the most recent year for which tax return information is available) is presented in Table 1. It compares the ratio of net income to total receipts in all industries, manufacturing, and the entire

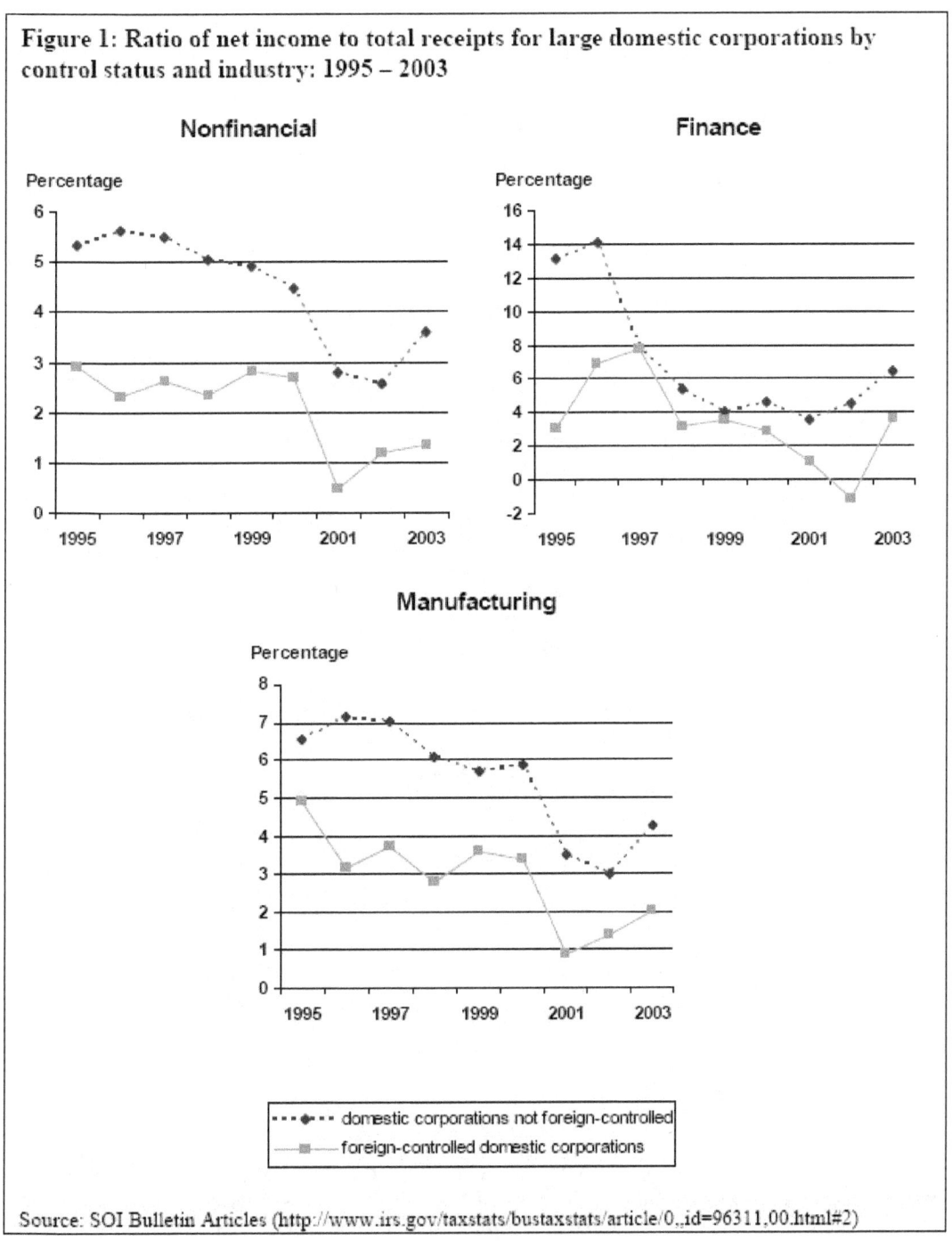

Figure 1: Ratio of net income to total receipts for large domestic corporations by control status and industry: 1995 – 2003

Nonfinancial

Finance

Manufacturing

- - - ◆ - - - domestic corporations not foreign-controlled
■ foreign-controlled domestic corporations

Source: SOI Bulletin Articles (http://www.irs.gov/taxstats/bustaxstats/article/0,,id=96311,00.html#2)

financial and nonfinancial sectors by ownership category.[3] As in Figure 1, profitability is expressed relative to total receipts rather than total assets or equity because of the historical book value (i.e., the value at the time of acquisition) and other problems associated with assets reported on the corporate tax return. Newly acquired assets generally have a higher book value than the assets they replaced. Comparisons using book value measures may be misleading if either FCDCs or DCCs contain a larger share of corporations with newly-acquired assets, such as new corporations. In addition, the balance sheet also includes foreign assets and liabilities, and furthermore corporations apparently vary on how these are stated, e.g., sometimes the foreign assets are on a gross basis and sometimes on a net equity basis. Also, corporations that file consolidated tax returns frequently do not net out intercompany assets and liabilities.

The three categories of corporations displayed in Table 1 are those that are more than 50 percent owned by foreigners, those with 25 to 50 percent foreign ownership, and all other corporations (referred to as domestically controlled). The estimated lower profitability of FCDCs compared with DCCs is evident in all industry groupings. For example, in manufacturing the ratio of net income to total receipts is about one-third lower for FCDCs (3.3 percent) than for DCCs (4.9 percent). The ratio of net income to total receipts is also substantially lower for FCDCs than for DCCs in the financial and nonfinancial sectors.

---

[3] Table 1 is based on tabulations of data from Form 1120, the corporate income tax return. They differ somewhat from the tabulations published by the Statistics of Income Division, which were used to construct Figure 1. Unlike Figure 1, Table 1 is not restricted to large corporations. Also, Table 1 defines FCDCs as corporations with greater than 50 percent foreign ownership, whereas Figure 1 uses 50 percent or more foreign ownership.

Table 1 — The Ratio of Net Income to Total Receipts and Number of Corporate Tax Returns by Ownership Category and Sector: 2004				
	All Industries	Manufacturing	All Nonfinancial	Financial
Ownership Category	Ratio of Net Income to Total Receipts (%)			
Foreign Ownership > 50%	2.9	3.3	2.8	3.9
Foreign Ownership 25 - 50%	3.0	4.9	2.9	6.1
Domestically Controlled	4.3	4.9	3.8	6.6
	Number of Corporate Returns in Sample			
Foreign Ownership > 50%	10,202	2,671	8,243	1,959
Foreign Ownership 25 - 50%	832	238	724	108
Domestically Controlled	65,550	10,197	52,638	12,912

Notes: These estimates are based on data from corporate income tax returns for 2004. They exclude REITs, RICs, Subchapter S Corporations, and branches of foreign corporations filing on 1120F. Number of returns is unweighted.

This paper explores the possible sources of the apparent discrepancy between the net income of foreign-controlled and domestically-controlled corporations, with a special attention to interest expense. Several explanations for the difference in profitability are possible, such as start up costs, a different structure of income and assets, and the distortion of transfer prices in intercompany transactions. The low relative profitability of foreign-controlled domestic corporations has been studied in the past by Grubert, Goodspeed and Swensen (1993), Grubert (1997) and Blouin, Collins and Shackelford (2001), among others. This paper updates some of these earlier studies for recent developments. It also extends the analysis in Grubert, Goodspeed and Swenson (1993) and Grubert (1997) to include the financial sector. The emphasis is on industries in which foreign-controlled domestic corporations are heavily represented, such as manufacturing and securities dealers and investment banks.

The study of the profitability of foreign-controlled domestic corporations in the United States raises the question of the appropriate "control" or comparison group for the analysis. The corporations in the 25 to 50 percent ownership category are a convenient comparison group because minority ownership would be expected to provide much fewer opportunities for income shifting. If they have profitability levels comparable to foreign-controlled domestic corporations, this might indicate that all foreign corporations tend to invest in similar U.S. corporations irrespective of ownership levels. (The overwhelming share of foreign-controlled domestic corporations in the United States are the product of acquisitions, not 'green field' startups.) However, the 25-50 percent owned category tends to be a small group of corporations and they cannot be consistently relied on for any firm conclusions, particularly at the industry level. Most of the discussion below, therefore, is based on a comparison of foreign-controlled and domestically-controlled corporations.

Some may claim that U.S. based multinational corporations (MNCs) should not be in the control group because they have many opportunities to shift income out of the United States as well. However, the group of domestic corporations with no foreign operations, in industries like manufacturing, may have special characteristics such as lower profitability and fewer intangible assets which limit their opportunities for investing abroad.

Grubert (1997) found that one factor explaining a substantial part of the differing net profitability of FCDCs and DCCs in the nonfinancial sector is that DCCs receive a substantial amount of dividends, interest, and royalties from foreign affiliates. Their observed net income, therefore, does not accurately reflect the profitability of their domestic operations alone. In order to isolate some of the more important factors that may explain differences in profitability, a measure of *operating income* is calculated for the two groups by subtracting interest, royalties and dividends received from net income, and adding back interest paid, depreciation, depletion and amortization. The objective is to obtain a measure of income that reflects the profitability of corporations' *domestic* operations. The denominator in the operating profits ratio, total receipts, is similar to domestic sales in the case of nonfinancial corporations.

Table 2 therefore constructs the ratio of operating income to total receipts for all nonfinancial corporations and for manufacturing corporations alone.[4] The first row for each category repeats the ratio of net income to total receipts from Table 1 and shows the large difference in profitability between foreign-controlled domestic corporations and domestically-controlled corporations. The next six rows present the income and expense components used to convert net income to operating income, all in relation to total receipts, for foreign-controlled and domestic corporations. There are substantial differences between the two groups. DCCs pay somewhat more interest in relation to total receipts but this is more than offset by the much larger amount of interest income they receive.[5] DCCs receive substantially more dividends and royalties than FCDCs. FCDCs and DCCs had similar depreciation deductions, with somewhat larger DCC deductions in the entire nonfinancial sector, but not in the manufacturing sector by itself.

The net result of adding and subtracting the various components is shown in the last row. The discrepancy in profitability between FCDCs and DCCs in the nonfinancial sector when net income is the profitability measure disappears. In the nonfinancial sector, FCDCs are slightly more profitable than DCCs in terms of operating income (6.3

---

[4] The same definition of operating earnings cannot be used in the financial sector. Interest income and expense and the spread they earn on them are an intrinsic part of their operations.
[5] The regressions below attempt to estimate the extent to which greater interest income creates the opportunity for greater borrowing.

Table 2
Net Income Adjusted to Operating Income
in the Nonfinancial and Manufacturing Sectors
by Ownership Category: 2004

	All Nonfinancial		
	Foreign Control	Foreign Ownership 25 - 50%	Domestic Control
Net Income / Total Receipts	2.8	2.9	3.8
Plus:			
Interest Paid / Total Receipts	3.1	1.8	3.8
Depreciation & Amortization / Total Receipts	4.2	3.9	4.4
Depletion / Total Receipts	0.1	0.1	0.1
Minus:			
Dividends Received / Total Receipts	0.5	0.5	1.2
Interest Received / Total Receipts	2.9	0.7	4.4
Royalties Received / Total Receipts	0.5	1.2	1.0
Operating Income / Total Receipts	6.3	6.3	5.5
	Manufacturing		
	Foreign Control	Foreign Ownership 25 - 50%	Domestic Control
Net Income / Total Receipts	3.3	4.9	4.9
Plus:			
Interest Paid / Total Receipts	2.4	2.3	3.2
Depreciation & Amortization / Total Receipts	4.3	5.0	4.0
Depletion / Total Receipts	0.1	0.0	0.1
Minus:			
Dividends Received / Total Receipts	0.4	0.7	2.1
Interest Received / Total Receipts	1.3	0.8	2.4
Royalties Received / Total Receipts	0.5	1.4	1.8
Operating Income / Total Receipts	7.9	9.3	5.9

Notes: Shares reported as percentages. Operating Income = Net Income + Interest Paid + Depreciation + Depletion - Dividends - Royalties - Interest Received. Estimates based on corporate income tax returns for 2004. Excludes RICs, REITs, and Subchapter S Corporations.

percent for FCDCs compared with 5.5 percent for DCCs). In manufacturing, FCDCs are significantly more profitable than DCCs on this basis (7.9 percent for FCDCs compared with 5.9 percent for DCCs). An important reason for these differences is that DCCs receive a greater amount of dividends and royalties relative to total receipts (which are subtracted in computing operating income), particularly in manufacturing where DCCs have significant foreign operations. On the basis of these aggregate data, FCDCs in the nonfinancial sector do not seem on average to be less profitable than DCCs when their operating incomes are compared. However, that still leaves open the question of leverage and interest expense, which is the reason they are the subject of much of the analysis below.

As noted later when the regression analysis is discussed, it might be claimed that royalties received should not be taken out of operating income because they represent the return to R&D and other expenses that have been deducted from taxable income. But even if royalties are kept in operating income, both Table 2 and the regression indicate that FCDC operating earnings continue to be greater than DCC earnings in relation to total receipts.

The higher profitability of FCDCs compared to DCCs when operating income is used as the profitability measure does not mean that FCDCs are not shifting income out of the United States. The comparison shown in Table 2 is at an aggregate level and may not account for systematic differences between foreign and domestic corporations at the level of the firm that may affect profitability.[6] Further, the domestic corporation control group itself also may be shifting income out of the United States. Grubert (1997) found that the translation from net income to operating income only eliminated about 60 percent of the initial gap in the ratio of net income to receipts in manufacturing in 1993. The adjustment is much more significant for 2004. The possibility that DCCs are shifting more income abroad is suggested by Figure 1, which shows that the ratio of net income to receipts of U.S. corporations in manufacturing declined substantially from 1995 to 2003.

---

[6]The statistical analysis presented below attempts to control for other factors that may affect profitability.

Section 163(j) is directed at taxpayers that have very high interest expense relative to cash flow. Whereas Table 2 provided information on average interest expense relative to total receipts, Table 3 presents the distribution of interest paid relative to cash flow by FCDCs and DCCs. The distributions are presented for all industries and separately for manufacturing, and the entire nonfinancial sector. A similar distribution of interest expense relative to cash flow in the financial sector (excluding insurance) is presented in Table 8 below in the separate section on financial industries.

Table 3 presents the percent of FCDC and DCC receipts and cash flow accounted for by corporations in selected intervals of the ratio of interest expense to cash flow. Cash flow is defined similarly to "adjusted income" in section 163(j): net income (before net operating loss deductions) plus interest paid, depreciation, depletion and amortization. The ratio differs from section 163(j) in that interest income is not netted from interest expense in the numerator.

Table 3 indicates that, in manufacturing and the nonfinancial sector as a whole, it is very difficult to identify major differences in the frequency of high interest expense. DCCs are somewhat more likely to have high interest expense in relation to cash flow. For example, in the manufacturing sector FCDCs with interest expense equal to 50 percent or more of cash flow accounted for 10.4 percent of their receipts (6.6 percent plus 3.8 percent) and 10.6 percent of their cash flow (7.9 percent plus 2.7 percent). In contrast, DCCs with interest expense equal to 50 percent or more of cash flow accounted for 13.7 percent of their receipts (8.8 percent plus 4.9 percent and 16.2 percent of their cash flow (14.0 percent plus 2.2 percent).

Table 3
Distribution of Interest Paid to Cash Flow by Percent of Total Receipts and Cash Flow for All Industries, Manufacturing and the Nonfinancial Sector: 2004

All Industries				
	Total Receipts		Cash Flow	
Interest Paid/Cash Flow	Foreign Control	Domestic Control	Foreign Control	Domestic Control
.00 ≤ ratio < .25	62.7	61.9	50.1	49.0
.25 ≤ ratio < .50	19.1	22.4	21.5	21.1
.50 ≤ ratio < .75	12.4	8.7	16.1	17.0
.75 or more	5.9	7.0	12.3	13.0
Total	100.0	100.0	100.0	100.0

Manufacturing				
	Total Receipts		Cash Flow	
Interest Paid/Cash Flow	Foreign Control	Domestic Control	Foreign Control	Domestic Control
.00 ≤ ratio < .25	69.3	61.1	62.7	62.4
.25 ≤ ratio < .50	20.3	25.2	26.6	21.5
.50 ≤ ratio < .75	6.6	8.8	7.9	14.0
.75 or more	3.8	4.9	2.7	2.2
Total	100.0	100.0	100.0	100.0

All Nonfinancial				
	Total Receipts		Cash Flow	
Interest Paid/Cash Flow	Foreign Control	Domestic Control	Foreign Control	Domestic Control
.00 ≤ ratio < .25	64.4	63.8	55.6	56.5
.25 ≤ ratio < .50	19.4	22.7	24.1	23.1
.50 ≤ ratio < .75	12.6	8.4	18.0	17.5
.75 or more	3.6	5.0	2.4	2.8
Total	100.0	100.0	100.0	100.0

Note: These estimates are based on data from corporate income tax returns for 2004. They exclude REITs, RICs, Subchapter S corporations, and branches of foreign corporations filing on Form 1120F and corporations in the 25-50% ownership category. The financial sector excludes insurance and real estate.

However, the comparison of FCDCs and DCCs in manufacturing with interest expense equal to 75 percent or more of cash flow yields a somewhat more mixed picture, with the result depending on whether the share of total receipts or the share of total cash flow is used as the criterion. Corporations with interest expense equal to 75 percent or more of cash flow account for 3.8 percent of FCDC receipts compared to 4.9 percent of DCC receipts. On the other hand, corporations with interest expense equal to 75 percent or more of total cash flow accounted for 2.7 percent of FCDC cash flow but only 2.2 percent of DCC cash flow.

In the nonfinancial sector as a whole, the comparison of FCDCs and DCCs with interest expense equal to 50 percent or more of cash flow also provides mixed results, depending on whether the share of total receipts or the share of cash flow is used as the criterion. The share of total receipts is 16.2 percent for FCDCs (12.6 percent plus 3.6 percent) and 13.4 percent for DCCs (8.4 percent plus 5.0 percent). However, the share of total cash flow is approximately the same for both FCDCs and DCCs: 20.4 percent for FCDCs (18.0 plus 2.4 percent) compared to 20.3 percent for DCCs (17.5 percent plus 2.8 percent). On the other hand, DCCs with interest expense of 75 percent or more of cash flow are more likely to have high interest expense than FCDCs using either total receipts or cash flow as the criterion.

Most of the remaining analysis of nonfinancial corporations is based on regressions and probit techniques using firm level data. These statistical techniques control for systematic differences between the groups of corporations that might cause their profitability and interest expense to vary. For example, profitability might be affected by corporate age and comparisons may be distorted because foreign-controlled domestic corporations are more recently established. Profitability in relation to sales may be influenced by how much the corporations purchase from others. A higher reliance on outside components means that they need less capital per unit of final sales. Similarly, in analyzing the use of debt, it is important to control for the composition of the corporation's assets because this could determine how much they can borrow. For example, they might be expected to be able to have greater leverage if they have a greater amount of cash and other very liquid assets instead of fixed depreciable plant and equipment.

One issue in using regressions in which the observations vary greatly in size is how the observations should be weighted. The ratio of net income to receipts is likely to exhibit much more variability (heteroskedasticity) in the case of small corporations than large corporations. Large observations, therefore, carry more information. One solution is to weight each observation in a given regression by the size of total receipts. In this paper, we first estimated the relation between the variance of the profit rate in a sector and the size of the corporations' gross receipts. In most cases, the size variable is the log of total receipts, but in a few cases the inverse of total receipts proved to be a better specification. In all cases the variability of the profit rate fell as the corporation became larger. The estimated relationship between size and variance was then used to form the weights in the final regression.[7]

While the results are generally consistent, it is necessary to distinguish between the questions answered by the aggregate data in Tables 1-3 and by the firm level regressions. The aggregate tables give an overall picture, as if all the corporations in a particular category were aggregated into a single firm. The regressions attempt to determine if there are statistically significant differences between FCDCS and DCCs after controlling for identifiable characteristics of each corporation. One reason why the answers may differ is because the aggregate data can be affected by extreme behavior by a limited number of firms, but they are too few and idiosyncratic to permit us to draw

---

[7] The weight for an observation was the inverse of the variance for a company of its size.

13

statistically reliable conclusions. For example, there may be a very large corporation that dominates the aggregate statistics but does not reveal enough about the "typical" corporation to permit general conclusions.[8]

As indicated earlier, the analysis first concentrates on nonfinancial corporations and then examines selected financial industries, such as investment banking and insurance, in the next section. Because of the special nature of finance, the data analysis must necessarily differ. For example, interest received may be passive portfolio income for a manufacturing corporation, but part of operating income for a bank.

Tables 4 and 5 present firm level regressions in which the dependent variables are the ratio of net income to total receipts and the ratio of operating income to total receipts in manufacturing and nonfinancial industries as a whole (excluding utilities), respectively.[9] Therefore, they complement the aggregate tabulations in Tables 1 and 2. The regressions use the same Statistics of Income Division sample of corporate returns for 2004. As in the aggregate tabulations in Tables 1 and 2, the sample excludes tax returns filed by subchapter S corporations, Regulated Investment Corporations (RICs), Real Estate Investment Trusts (REITs) and branches of foreign corporations. In addition, corporations with assets below $50 million are excluded.[10]

In Tables 4 and 5, for corporations in manufacturing and the entire nonfinancial sector, respectively, the first column of results relates the ratio of net income to total receipts to dummy variables for the two basic foreign ownership categories, greater than

---

[8] In the regressions, some observations are deleted, for example, if there are no assets or sales for the company in the data file.

[9] Utilities are excluded from the nonfinancial sector in the regressions because of the special features of rate regulated industries, such as the ability to issue a large amount of debt.

[10] The exclusion of corporations with less than $50 million in assets supplements the weighting scheme to keep the conclusions from being unduly influenced by small idiosyncratic corporations.

50 percent and 25 to 50 percent. They therefore parallel the net income tabulations in Table 1 and yield similar results on the discrepancy between FCDCs and DCCs. For example, Table 1 shows that in manufacturing, the profit rate of FCDCs is 1.4 percentage points lower than the 4.3 percent of sales earned by DCCs. The coefficient of the FCDC variable in the first regression on Table 4 indicates that FCDCs on average have a profit rate 1.4 percentage points below the rate of profits on sales earned by DCCs and that the sample mean is 4.3 percent.

The second column of results in Tables 4 and 5 analyzes how much the estimated differential between FCDCs and DCCs in the first column, the FCDC coefficient, is explained by systematic differences between the corporations. The four added explanatory variables are two age categories, based on the date of incorporation, the ratio of purchases to sales and the ratio of total assets to total receipts. The age variables test the possibility that some of the net income discrepancy between FCDCs and DCCs is attributable to start-up costs by relatively immature FCDCs.[11] The ratio of purchases to sales adjusts for the possibility that corporations that rely more on outside supplies can be expected to have a lower profit margin on total receipts because they need less of their own capital. The purpose of the fourth variable, the ratio of assets to sales, is to adjust for the fact that net income is expressed relative to receipts, rather than assets, which would be closer to a rate of return measure. As in the aggregate tabulations, total receipts are chosen for the denominator because of the uncertainty over what corporations put on the balance sheet reported on their tax return, even apart from the standard historical

---

[11] A recent incorporation date may indicate a recent acquisition or merger, not an actual start up.

book valuation problems in asset accounts.[12] Nevertheless, the ratio of total assets to total receipts is added as an indicator of capital intensity because of the possibility that the total asset data do contain some information, albeit flawed.

Independent Variables	Dependent Variables		
	Net Income / Total Reciepts	Net Income / Total Reciepts	Operating Income / Total Receipts
Foreign Ownership > 50 percent	-.0140**	-.0058	.0095**
	(4.20)	(1.76)	(3.02)
Foreign Ownership 25-50 percent	.0120	.0117	.0175
	(1.15)	(1.15)	(1.82)
Age < 5 years		-.0314**	-.0008
		(7.24)	(0.20)
Age 5 - 15 years		-.0146**	.0007
		(4.10)	(0.22)
Purchases / Sales		-.0773**	-.1173**
		(10.25)	(16.47)
Assets / Sales		.0009	.00003
		(0.91)	(0.04)
Mean of dependent variable	.0433	.0433	.0854
Number of observations	3087	3087	3087

Table 4
Manufacturing, 2004
Regressions for Net Income & Operating Income

Notes:
1) Operating income is net income minus interest income, dividends and royalties, interest paid, depreciation, depletion, and amortization.
2) t values are in parentheses.
3) Companies with total assets less than $50 million are excluded from the sample.
4) ** means significant at the 1 percent level

The second column of results in both Tables 4 and 5 indicate that these added variables seem to explain a substantial portion of the initial FCDC-DCC discrepancy in the ratio of net income to total receipts. Indeed, the initial negative coefficients for FCDCs in the first column shrink by more than half in the second column. The

---

[12]As discussed earlier, one issue is how assets in subsidiaries abroad are reported. The use of total receipts, which are dominated by sales in the case of nonfinancial corporations, largely abstracts from this by focusing only on the operations of the company in the United States.

coefficients for the age dummies and the purchases variable have the expected negative

signs and are statistically significant. Adding the purchases variable has a particularly

significant impact on the FCDC coefficient.

	Table 5 Nonfinancial Sector, 2004 Regressions for Net Income & Operating Income		
Independent Variables	**Dependent Variables**		
	Net Income / Total Reciepts	**Net Income / Total Reciepts**	**Operating Income / Total Receipts**
Foreign Ownership > 50 percent	-.0145**	-.0031	.0182**
	(6.21)	(1.34)	(5.21)
Foreign Ownership 25-50 percent	-.0025	-.0057	.0298**
	(0.32)	(0.73)	(2.58)
Age < 5 years		-.0335**	.0058
		(11.60)	(1.35)
Age 5 - 15 years		-.0164**	.0004
		(7.23)	(0.10)
Purchases / Sales		-.0620**	-.0124*
		(18.91)	(2.52)
Assets / Sales		.00003**	.000010
		(4.12)	(0.93)
Mean of dependent variable	.0477	.0477	.0648
Number of observations	8185	8185	8185

Notes:
1) Operating income is net income minus interest income, dividends and royalties, interest paid, depreciation, depletion, and amortization.
2) t values are in parentheses.
3) Companies with total assets less than $50 million are excluded from the sample.
4) * means significant at the 5 percent level and ** means significant at the 1 percent level.

The last column of results in Tables 4 and 5 substitutes the ratio of operating

income to total receipts as the income measure. Operating income, as in Table 2, is

defined as net income *plus* interest paid, depreciation, depletion and amortization and

minus interest, royalties and dividends received. Its main purpose is to remove financial

income such as dividends and royalties, which mainly come from foreign affiliates, so that the income measure reflects purely domestic operations. As in Table 2, the use of operating income as the income measure results in a positive FCDC coefficient in Tables 4 and 5, indicating higher operating profitability by FCDCs.

The regressions in Table 4 for net income suggested that the age of the corporations and their reliance on outside suppliers explained a large part of the profitability differential between FCDCs and DCCs. But these factors become insignificant when operating income is used as the profitability measure. This suggests that the age variables and the importance of purchased materials tend to indicate immature corporations that are less likely to receive dividends and royalties from their foreign operations.

It might justifiably be argued that royalties should be included in domestic operating income because it represents the return to domestic R&D, which is deductible from U.S. taxable income. However, additional regressions (not shown) indicate that removing dividends from net income is enough to eliminate the foreign differential in the regressions with the explanatory variables that are used in columns 2 and 3. Furthermore, the greater amount of royalties that DCCs receive from abroad probably indicates that they have many more U.S. developed intangibles that can be applied to domestic production.

Regressions, not shown in the tables, for the separate components of operating income show the reasons for the difference between the net income and operating income comparisons. In manufacturing, the greater amount of dividends and royalties received by domestically-controlled corporations is particularly notable. This reflects the large amount of foreign income the domestically-controlled manufacturing corporations receive from their foreign operations.

Tables 6 and 7 analyze interest expense relative to cash flow in manufacturing and in the entire nonfinancial sector. Interest expense is expressed in relation to cash flow, in part, because that is the ratio used in section 163(j). Prospective lenders would be expected to use the extent to which interest payments are covered by cash flow in judging the corporation's creditworthiness. However, explanatory variables are added that provide more detail on the corporations' assets and operations and give a clearer picture of the determinants of the amount they borrow. For example, if a nonfinancial corporation receives a great deal of interest, this might indicate that it has a substantial financial component and is more likely to be highly leveraged. It might also be easier to borrow on the basis of very liquid assets compared to fixed plant and equipment.

Before discussing the interest expense results in Tables 6 and 7, it is appropriate to consider how a corporation's interest expense might be related to these variables. The relationship is not entirely straightforward, because the extent to which a corporation incurs interest expense reflects both the credit that is available from lenders and the corporation's own financial strategy as it evolves. Furthermore, stating that the optimal strategy is simply a matter of leveraging up until bankruptcy risks increase the after-tax cost of debt to the cost of equity leaves open the issue of the cost of retained earnings.[13] The role of cash on the balance sheet is a notable example of this complicated relationship. Lenders would be very willing to extend credit to cash laden firms but the presence of cash on the balance sheet is itself a reflection of the corporation's financial decisions over time. The corporation may be very profitable and it may not choose to

---

[13]See Brys and Bovenberg (2006).

take full advantage of its borrowing power because that would require huge taxable dividends to shareholders. Paying off debt and accumulating liquid assets may be a preferred strategy.

Table 6 provides regressions in which the dependent variable is the ratio of interest expense to cash flow and Table 7 presents probit analyses for the likelihood that a corporation with given characteristics has interest expense greater than 50 percent of cash flow, the section 163(j) threshold. As in Table 3, cash flow is defined as net income plus interest paid plus depreciation, depletion and amortization. In addition to the age and foreign control variables, the explanatory variables in the Table 6 regressions include: (1) the distribution of total assets among cash, notes and accounts receivable, government and tax exempt securities, inventories and depreciable capital, (2) the ratio of interest received to cash flow, (3) corporate size, defined as the log of total receipts, (4) loans from shareholders as a percent of total assets and (5) the interaction of the loans from shareholder variable with the identifier of foreign control.[14]

The asset composition variables are included because some assets can be much easier to use as explicit or implicit collateral. The interest received variable is introduced to identify those nonfinancial corporations that have a large financial operation with greater opportunities for leverage. A measure of corporate size is included because larger corporations may be able to borrow more capital. Alternatively, large mature corporations may have less need for borrowing. (As suggested above, the amount of observed borrowing reflects both the behavior of prospective lenders and the demand for

---

[14] In Tables 6 and 7 corporations with 25 to 50 percent foreign ownership are included with DCCs. They are presumably in most cased domestically controlled and, in any case, are not in a position to shift income to related parties abroad. The earlier tables indicate that they are too small a group to be relied on for any significant conclusions. Deleting them from the sample would not make much of a difference.

financing by the borrower.) Loans from shareholders are included because such loans may offer the corporation a greater opportunity for having more total debt. The interaction of shareholder loans with the foreign control variable indicates whether FCDCs in particular take advantage of shareholder borrowing to achieve greater total borrowing.

The foreign control coefficients in Table 6 indicate that FCDCs in manufacturing and in the nonfinancial sector have smaller interest expense relative to cash flow than DCCs. In the nonfinancial sector as a whole, FCDCs pay almost 3 percentage points less of cash flow in interest than DCCs and in manufacturing the differential is more than 6 percentage points.

The results in Table 6 for the other explanatory variables show that recently incorporated corporations have a greater ratio of interest expense to cash flow. This might reflect leveraging up after a reincorporation associated with a merger or acquisition. Also, the amount of interest income relative cash flow is very strongly associated with greater interest expense. This could be attributable to financial operations that are part of the corporation identified as being principally nonfinancial. It could reflect liquid assets that are easier to leverage.

Another possible explanation is the feature of the section 163(j) rules that permit the netting of interest received from interest expense before calculating whether any interest is nondeductible. Corporations with a great deal of cash on their balance sheet have significantly lower interest expense, presumably because the cash indicates that they do not have much need for debt finance. Finally, the negative coefficients for the interaction of foreign control and loans from shareholders indicate that, FCDCs are less likely to use these loans as an opportunity to increase total borrowing than DCCs.

Whereas the Table 6 regressions examine the interest paid by FCDCs in manufacturing and the entire nonfinancial sector on *average*, the probit equations in Table 7, similar to regressions but applicable when a bifurcated frequency is studied, examine whether the frequency of extremely high interest expense relative to cash flow is greater for foreign-controlled corporations. These corporations are presumably the potential targets of a thin capitalization or interest stripping policy. The threshold chosen in Table 7 is 50 percent of cash flow, as in section 163(j) except that interest income is not netted from interest expense in the denominator for the purposes of calculating the ratio. The independent variables in Table 7 are the ones like the ratio of interest received to cash flow that were most significant in Table 6 or were of special interest like the amount of related party loans. The probit analyses in Table 7 indicate that foreign FCDCs in manufacturing and the entire nonfinancial sector are *less* likely to have interest expense in excess of 50 percent of cash flow than DCCs.[15] (Other probits, not displayed, show that FCDCs are also less likely than DCCs to have interest expense greater than 75 percent of cash flow.) The fact that FCDCs are less likely to be above the threshold may reflect the impact of section 163(j). The impact of the other variables is generally similar to Table 6. Recently incorporated corporations are more likely to have interest payments in excess of 50 percent of cash flow.

---

[15] The observations are not weighed in the probit analyses because heteroskedasticity is less of an issue for bifurcated 0 or 1 dependent variables.

Table 6
Nonfinancial Sector and Manufacturing, 2004
The Ratio of Interest Paid to Cash Flow

Independent Variables	Manufacturing	Nonfinancial Sector
Foreign Ownership > 50 percent	-.0643**	-.0278**
	(3.03)	(2.77)
Age < 5 years	.2470**	.1647**
	(9.04)	(13.37)
Age 5 - 15 years	.1085**	.0772**
	(4.92)	(8.12)
Depreciable Assets / Total Assets	-.0805	-.1066**
	(1.33)	(4.32)
Inventories / Total Assets	-.0825	-.1757**
	(0.96)	(5.39)
Cash / Total Assets	-.9570**	-.6739**
	(10.88)	(18.18)
Interest Income / Cash flow	1.0407**	.3519**
	(17.60)	(25.12)
Notes + Accounts Receivable / Total Assets	-.2392**	-.2533**
	(3.17)	(10.27)
Government Securities / Total Assets	-.9652**	-.7874**
	(2.76)	(8.55)
Purchases / Sales	.1020*	.0850**
	(2.09)	(4.79)
Loans from Shareholders / Total Assets	.8908*	.5068**
	(2.18)	(3.79)
Foreign Control X Loans from Shareholders / Total Assets	-.8219	-.3194*
	(1.89)	(2.11)
Size: Log of Total Receipts	-.0133*	-.0055*
	(1.97)	(2.05)
Mean of dependent variable	.3132	.2859
Number of observations	3087	8185

Notes:
1) Cash flow is equal to net income plus interest paid plus depreciation, depletion, and amortization.
2) Weights as in Tables 4 and 5.
3) t values are in parentheses.
4) Companies with less than $50 million in assets excluded from sample.
5) * means significant at the 5 percent level and ** means significant at the 1 percent level.

Table 7
Nonfinancial Sector and Manufacturing, 2004
Probit Analysis: The Probability that a Company has Interest Paid
Greater than 50 Percent of Cash Flow

Independent Variables	Manufacturing	Nonfinancial Sector
Foreign Ownership > 50 percent	-.2630**	-0954*
	(3.83)	(2.13)
Age < 5 years	.7800**	.5885**
	(10.12)	(12.39)
Age 5 - 15 years	.4319**	.3400**
	(6.18)	(8.42)
Cash / Total Assets	-4.637**	-3.301**
	(8.76)	(12.78)
Interest Income / Cash Flow	2.596**	1.008**
	(15.25)	(27.24)
Purchases / Sales	.2284	.0862
	(1.52)	(1.31)
Size of Company: Log of Total Receipts	-.0019	-.0049
	(0.09)	(0.42)
Loans from Shareholders / Total Assets	1.992	2.001**
	(1.86)	(4.17)
Foreign Control X Loans from Shareholders / Total Assets	-1.169	-1.172*
	(-1.02)	(-2.14)
Mean Likelihood	0.1701	0.2004

Notes to table:
1) t values are in parentheses.
2) Companies with total assets less than $50 million are excluded from the sample.
3) Observations in probits are unweighted.
4) Cash flow is defined as in Table 6.
5) * means significant at the 5 percent level and ** means significant at the 1 percent level.

Greater interest income is very significant in pushing corporations over the threshold. Furthermore, the coefficient of the interaction of the FCDC dummy variable with loans from shareholders indicates that FCDCs are less likely than DCCs to use shareholder loans to be able to have 'excess' interest expense.

The Financial Sector

Because the financial sector is very heterogeneous, several industries are examined separately: commercial banks, brokers and investment banks, stock life insurance, stock property and casualty insurance, and real estate. Foreign corporations in each of these industries vary a great deal in terms of how their profitability and leverage compare to their domestically-controlled counterparts. For example, commercial bank FCDCs had a slightly lower ratio of net income to total revenue than DCC commercial banks, but any discrepancy seems largely attributable to the greater amount of dividends that DCC banks receive. However, the profitability differential between FCDC and DCC securities dealers and investment banks was substantial in 2004, with net income equal to 4.2 percent of revenues for FCDCs compared to 7.1 percent earned by DCCs, and a wide disparity was also notable in 2002 and 2003, the other years examined in detail. Stock life insurance FCDCs had profits similar to their DCC counterparts in 2004 (as well as in 2002 and 2003). However, stock property and casualty FCDCs were much less profitable than DCCs in 2004, when net income was equal to1.4 percent of revenues for the former versus 6.4 percent for the latter. The FCDCs in property and casualty insurance also made large losses in 2002 when DCCs were profitable and they had meager profits compared to DCCs in 2003. Finally, FCDCs in real estate were much more profitable than comparable DCCs in each of the three years and they also had much less debt.

In the financial sector, corporations generally have much greater leverage than in the nonfinancial sector. Therefore, in Table 8 which parallels Table 3 in presenting the distribution of the ratio of interest to cash flow for FCDCs and DCCs , a threshold ratio of interest expense to cash flow of 90 percent, rather than the 50 percent threshold used above for nonfinancial corporations, may be a more appropriate measure of high interest expense. The distribution of interest paid to cash flow in Table 8 shows that FCDCs do seem to be more likely to have very high levels of interest expense relative to cash flow, but the comparison is not completely unambiguous.[16]   Table 8 indicates that corporations

with interest expense of 90 percent or more of cash flow account for 50.3 percent of total

FCDC receipts compared to 24.3 percent of total DCC receipts, and 53.7 percent of total

FCDC cash flow compared to 37.4 of DCC cash flow. FCDCs in finance are also much

more likely to have interest expense greater than or equal to cash flow, measured either in

terms of the share of total receipts or cash flow. However, a greater share of receipts and

cash flow are above the 95 percent threshold for DCCs than for FCDCs. A significant

share of DCC receipts and cash flow fall in the 95 to 100 percent category.[17]

	Table 8 Distribution of Interest Paid Relative to Cash Flow by Percent of Total Receipts and Cash Flow for the Financial Sector: 2004			
	Financial			
	Total Receipts		Cash Flow	
Interest Paid/Cash Flow	Foreign Control	Domestic Control	Foreign Control	Domestic Control
.00 ≤ ratio < .25	16.7	18.5	16.7	9.5
.25 ≤ ratio < .50	9.1	16.4	6.5	10.8
.50 ≤ ratio < .75	5.0	15.2	5.2	14.5
.75 or more	69.1	49.9	71.6	65.3
i. .75 ≤ ratio < .90	18.8	25.6	17.9	27.9
ii. .90 ≤ ratio < .95	37.9	4.8	39.1	6.1
iii. .95 ≤ ratio < 1.0	1.4	18.0	2.5	29.7
iv. ratio ≥ 1	11.0	1.5	12.1	1.6
Total	100.0	100.0	100.0	100.0

Note: These estimates are based on data from corporate income tax returns for 2004. They exclude REITs, RICs, Subchapter S corporations, and branches of foreign corporations filing on Form 1120F and corporations in the 25-50% ownership category. The financial sector excludes insurance and real estate.

---

[16] We exclude insurance corporations from finance for this purpose because they are likely to have a much different relationship between interest expense and cash flow than other financial intermediaries.

[17] Corporations in finance tend not to be constrained by 163(j) because they can net interest income from interest paid. Because financial intermediaries earn an interest spread, they can frequently have negative *net* interest expense.

Tables 9 and 10 examine the profitability and interest expense issues in greater detail using firm level regressions and probits. Table 9 provides profitability regressions for selected financial industries which are similar to the regressions for the nonfinancial sector in Tables 4 and 5. The selected financial industries are the following: (1) commercial banks, (2) securities dealers and investment banks, (3) stock life insurance, (4) stock property and casualty insurance, and (5) real estate. In each regression, the dependent variable is the ratio of net income (line 28 on the Form 1120) to total revenue. The independent variables are the two age dummy variables and the two foreign ownership categories, greater than 50 percent and 25 to 50 percent.[18] In each case, as in Tables 4 and 5, the weights for the observations are based on the relationship between the variance of the profit ratio and the size of total receipts.

Table 9 shows that foreign-controlled domestic commercial banks are slightly less profitable than domestically-controlled banks, but the differential is neither very large nor statistically significant. The greater amount of dividends, not displayed explicitly on the table, that DCCs receive seems to account for any differential. Foreign-controlled domestic securities dealers and investment banks seem particularly unprofitable compared to DCCs. Indeed, the large (in absolute value) negative coefficient indicates that they are barely profitable when compared to the weighted industry mean of 7.1 percent of total receipts. (Other data, not displayed, show that foreign-controlled brokers and investment bankers also seem very unprofitable in terms of the ratio of net income to total assets.)

---

[18] The ratio of purchases to sales and the ratio of sales to assets used in the nonfinancial regressions in Table 4 and 5 are less relevant for financial corporations.

Table 9 indicates that foreign-controlled domestic real estate corporations are much more profitable than domestically-controlled real estate corporations. (Other data, not displayed, show that they are also much less highly leveraged.) Foreign-controlled domestic life insurance corporations are very close to DCC life insurance corporations in terms of net income as a percent of total revenue, with only a small and statistically insignificant coefficient. However, the regression for FCDC property and casualty insurance corporations shows that they were significantly less profitable than comparable DCCs, with a negative coefficient greater than 50 percent of the weighted industry mean.

Table 9
Profitability Regressions for Selected Financial Industries and Real Estate, 2004
(Dependent variable is the ratio of net income to total receipts)

Independent Variables	Commercial Banks	Securities Dealers & Investment Banks	Stock Life Insurance	Stock P&C Insurance	Real Estate
Foreign Ownership > 50 percent	-.0274 (1.64)	-.0664** (3.64)	-.0048 (0.47)	-.0357** (2.60)	.1235** (4.34)
Foreign Ownership 25-50 percent	-.0164 (0.30)	.0340 (0.14)	-.0597 (0.18)	.0710 (1.03)	-.0477 (0.15)
Age ≤ 5 years	-.0729** (6.20)	-.0076 (0.39)	.0908 (1.43)	-.1016** (3.31)	.0499 (1.30)
Age 5 - 15 years	-.0094 (0.60)	.0727** (2.70)	-.0224 (0.56)	-.0251 (1.46)	.0331 (1.17)
Mean of dependent variable	.1820	.0706	.0467	.0671	.0775
Number of observations	731	94	272	406	446

Notes:
1) Companies with assets less than $50 million excluded.
2) Observations are weighted based on the relationship between the variance of profitability and company size.
3) t values are in parentheses.
4) ** means significant at the 1 percent level.

In order to supplement the distributions of the ratio of interest expense to cash flow in the financial sector shown in Table 3, Table 10 focuses on the frequency of very high interest expense in relation to cash flow in commercial banking and in securities dealing and investment banking. The threshold used is interest expense that is greater than 90 percent of cash flow. Thus Table 10 presents probit equations that can be used to calculate the probability that a bank or broker with given characteristics will pay interest greater than the 90 percent of cash flow threshold. The equations include explanatory

Table 10
Probits: Probability that Interest Paid is Greater than 90 Percent of Cash Flow
Commercial Banks & Investment Banks and Securities Dealers, 2004

Independent Variables	Commercial Banks	Security Dealers and Investment Banks
Foreign Ownership > 50 percent	1.096**	1.32**
	(2.59)	(2.72)
Age < 5 years	.1949	-.0163
	(0.85)	(0.03)
Age 5 - 15 years	.1188	.3843
	(0.39)	(0.74)
Cash / Total Assets	-1.451	-.5610
	(0.94)	(0.27)
Interest Income / Cash Flow	.7321**	.7856*
	(8.45)	(2.05)
Size of Company: Log of Total Receipts	-.4800**	.2161*
	(2.71)	(2.32)
U.S. Government Obligations / Total Assets	-1.697*	1.305
	(2.03)	(0.45)
Tax Exempt Securities / Total Assets	-.0584	--
	-0.03	
Number of Observations	731	94
Mean Likelihood	.0561	.2021

Notes to table:
1) Companies with assets less than $50 million excluded.
2) t values are in parentheses.
3) Companies with foreign ownership between 25 and 50 percent are included in domestic controlled.
4) -- means too few held for valid estimation.
5) * means sigificant at the 5 percent level and ** means significant at the 1 percent level.

variables such as the amount of cash and government bonds on the balance sheet in order to control for the possibility that some financial businesses may be able to have much higher levels of debt because of the nature of their assets and operations.

Table 10 shows that FCDCs in both commercial banking and securities dealing and investment banking are much more likely to have interest expense greater than 90 percent of cash flow than comparable DCCs. The differential seems particularly notable for securities dealers and investment banks, a sector in which a much greater percent of the corporations are above the threshold than in commercial banking. For example, translating the probit equation in Table 10 into probabilities shows that the probability that a *domestically-controlled* securities dealer or investment bank pays more than 90 percent of cash flow in interest is less than 5 percent but more than 40 percent in the case of comparable foreign-controlled domestic corporations.

Conclusions

The analysis above indicates that in the *nonfinancial* sector foreign-controlled domestic corporations are *not* less profitable than their domestically-controlled counterparts when net income is adjusted for interest expense and investment income so that the income from U.S. *domestic* operations, before interest expense, can be more accurately compared. Much of the investment income that domestically-controlled corporations receive, particularly dividends and royalties, is from their affiliates abroad. FCDCs in the nonfinancial sector on the average have a lower ratio of interest expense to cash flow than comparable DCCs. They are also less likely to have interest expense that is greater than 50 percent of cash flow.

Foreign-controlled domestic corporations in the financial sector and real estate exhibited a wide range in relative profitability. Foreign-controlled domestic real estate corporations are much more profitable than comparable domestically-controlled corporations. Foreign-controlled domestic life insurance corporations are not significantly different from domestically-controlled stock corporations in profitability. However, foreign-controlled domestic property and casualty corporations were much less profitable than domestically-controlled corporations in 2004. (They made very large losses in 2004 when DCCs were profitable and they made modest profits compared to DCCs in 2003.)

Foreign-controlled domestic commercial banks were slightly less profitable than comparable domestically-controlled banks in 2004, although this seemed largely attributable to the greater amount of dividends domestic banks received. FCDC securities brokers and investment banks were much less profitable than comparable DCCs, barely profitable in 2004 as well as in 2002 and 2003. They were also much more likely to have extremely high levels of interest expense relative to cash flow. For example, the probability that a foreign-controlled domestic securities dealer or investment bank pays more than 90 percent of cash flow in interest is greater than 40 percent but less than 5 percent in the case of domestically-controlled corporations.

References

Blouin, Jennifer, Julie Collins, and Douglas Shackelford (2001), "Does Acquisition by Non-U.S. Shareholders Cause U.S. Firms to Pay less Tax?" presented at the International Seminar on Public Economics Conference on Income Taxation and Financial Innovation, Berkley, December 2001.

Brys, Bert, and Lans Bovenberg (2006), "The Life Cycle of the Firm with Debt and Capital Income Taxes," CentER Discussion Paper No. 2006-91.

Grubert, Harry, Timothy Goodspeed, and Deborah Swensen (1993), "Explaining the Low Taxable Income of Foreign-Controlled Corporations in the United States," in Studies in International Taxation, edited by Alberto R. Giovannini, R.Glenn Hubbard, and Joel Slemrod, 237-70, Chicago: Chicago University Press, 1993.

Grubert, Harry (1997), "Another Look at the Low Taxable Income of Foreign-Controlled Corporations in the United States," Office of Tax Analysis Paper 74, Department of the Treasury, October.